Silhouettes in America, 1790–1840

A Collectors' Guide

Blume J. Rifken

R Thayer
5/88

PARADIGM PRESS, INC.
Burlington, Vermont

ISBN: 0-943741-00-9
Library of Congress Catalog Card No.: 87–061986

Printing (last digit): 5 4 3 2 1

Paradigm Press, Inc.
PO Box 4422
Burlington, Vermont 05402

Cover and interior design by David E. Robinson
Typesetting by PostScript, Inc.
Illustrations by Blume J. Rifken
Photographs by Rhys Roberts

Printed in the United States

Contents

Foreword

SINCE THE LATE 1700s the art of the silhouettist has been much admired and collected. The first silhouettes were kept by the families or acquaintances of the subjects of the profiles.

The collecting of silhouettes as an art form can be traced back nearly 150 years in America. By the 1920s when the magazine *Antiques* began publication, there was sufficient interest and collecting activity for nearly every issue to contain at least one major article relating to the silhouette field. Several early writers in the areas of Americana also focused on silhouettes. The most comprehensive book, *Shades of Our Ancestors* by Alice Van Leer Carrick, was released in 1928.

Until now there has been an unfulfilled need for an in-depth guide to assist the collector in learning about the refinements of silhouette collecting. *Silhouettes in America, 1790–1840: A Collectors' Guide* by Blume Rifken is a teaching guide that serves this purpose. It emphasizes the development of a discerning eye. It contains information that will assist in the authentication and dating of early profiles. It also includes a chapter on conservation and preservation by the well-known conservator, C. R. Jones, who is associated with the New York State Historical Association at Cooperstown.

Many books of this type feature pieces from museum collections because the photographs are most easily obtained from cultural institutions. In this book you will find a large number of examples from private collections. This would seem to indicate that silhouettes are still relatively abundant in the marketplace and can be easily and inexpensively acquired by collectors.

This is a book from which to learn and be encouraged.

Dr. Robert Bishop, Director
Museum of American Folk Art
New York, New York

Preface

AS A COLLECTOR of American antique silhouettes of 1790 to 1840, I have often been disappointed in my pursuit of authentic, good-quality silhouettes. Not long ago, such silhouettes were difficult to find. Many dealers in otherwise high-quality Americana hadn't sufficient knowledge about silhouettes to buy them or stock them confidently.

At a highly regarded antique show, for example, a dealer who had for sale a mediocre "hollow-cut" silhouette told me that the method of cutting was quite unusual. In fact, the cutting style of his sample was the most common! At another show of equal quality, I found high-priced silhouettes in poor condition. I attribute these and similar errors to the lack of information about silhouettes.

Today silhouettes are noticeably more available at fine antique shows and are widely advertised by dealers. Yet many potential collectors are wary of buying them. These collectors need a guide on how to identify authentic, high-quality profiles that are legitimate antiques and how to avoid mediocre silhouettes or reproductions. I hope that this book, with its well-detailed photographs and helpful commentary, will serve this purpose.

Blume J. Rifken
June, 1987

Acknowledgments

I AM VERY GRATEFUL for the efforts of Rhys Roberts and his camera, Chuck Wainwright and his darkroom, David Robinson and his editing skills, Philip Frankel and his legal expertise, my encouraging family members and friends, and the generous people who allowed their silhouettes to be photographed for inclusion in this book.

Introduction

SHADOWS, SILHOUETTES, SHADES, PROFILES—these are all names for the basic, usually solid black, profiles of people from the past as well as our own friends and family members. Silhouette portraits have been a part of American life for many generations.

Through its photographs, this book illustrates the wide variety of styles and techniques among silhouette artists—from folk art to academic and all shades in between. The silhouettes shown in this book come from the period between 1790 and the 1840s, when this form of portraiture was most popular. During that time, many silhouette artists traveled the Northeast and South and found countless eager subjects for their art.

Silhouettes became popular in Europe in the mid-1700s, and the first American silhouette appeared considerably earlier than 1790. In *A History of American Silhouettes: A Collector's Guide—1790–1840*, Alice Van Leer Carrick quotes the following letter, written in South Carolina By Harriott Pinckney in 1769:

My dear Miss R ____:
Thos. Wollaston has summon'd me today, to put the finishing strokes to my Shadow, which straightens me for time.

To my knowledge, this is the earliest American silhouette reference.

The term *silhouette* derives from Etienne de Silhouette, an eighteenth-century French minister of finance who was very frugal in his fiscal policies. He was also an amateur profile portraitist. Because his critics thought him cheap, they referred to these very inexpensive personal likenesses as *silhouette* portraits. The name stuck, and it became widely used in this country after the arrival of the French silhouettist, Augustin Edouart.

Though inexpensive, silhouettes also had an enthusiastic following among the famous and affluent. Following a successful European career, Augustin Edouart came to the United States in 1839 and during the next ten years produced cuttings of a great many Americans who were prominent in business and politics.

Silhouettists: Good Artists, Good Salesmen

As mentioned earlier, most silhouette artists were itinerant, moving from city to city and taking up temporary residences to ply their trade. They advertised extensively in local papers or posted notices of their accomplishments around town.

From the sound of these posters or broadsides, silhouette artists were anything but humble—they used numerous boasts, ploys, and gimmicks to entice the public into their studios. Some artists advertised special exhibits of their work, calling them "Papyrotomia." Others invited patrons to a concert by a machine known as a Panharmonicum that they claimed could imitate the sounds of 206 musical instruments. Many artists put on quite a show.

Often people would read in an ad that the artist was residing in town for a very limited time, only to find in the next ad that he was extending his stay. This uncertainty about the artist's travel plans helped, no doubt, to draw business. It is obvious that the silhouettist not only had to be a good artist and craftsman but a good salesman as well.

Among the more talented silhouette artists of the period who worked in America were Charles Wilson Peale, William M. S. Doyle, Henry Williams, Todd, William King, William Bache, Master Hubard, Master Hankes, Augustin Edouart, William Henry Brown, T. P. Jones, William Chamberlain, Samuel Metford, and Rufus Porter. Some were natives and others traveled here from abroad.

There were also severely handicapped silhouettists who managed to provide an income for themselves by cutting profiles. The most famous was Miss M. A. Honeywell, who worked from 1806 to 1848. She had no hands, stumps for arms, and only one foot with three toes. She did her cuttings with a scissors held in her mouth, aided by one of her stumps. She signed her work "cut with the mouth" or a similar phrase. What a remarkable woman she must have been!

Silhouette Collecting Then and Now

Numerous advertisements by early silhouette artists mention the thousands of profiles they have made during their years of traveling—so many that a modern collector might expect today's dealers to be buried under silhouettes. Yet they are not. Many of the silhouettes one does find are poor to average in quality, and fine silhouettes take searching out. What has happened to all these profiles? Most likely many of them were never framed; they therefore were lost, damaged, or discarded by later generations who did not appreciate this early form of portraiture.

This neglect fortunately changed over the years, and by the 1920s, silhouette collecting had become quite popular. *Antiques* magazine had articles on silhouettes issue after issue. Today, after several decades of decline, interest in collecting silhouettes is reviving.

Besides silhouettes, miniature profile portraits in color were also popular in the Twenties. Some authorities proposed to group the silhouettes with these colored portraits, calling them all "portraits in profile." This proposal never caught on, probably because the term *silhouette* accurately describes a distinctive type of profile: a solid-cut form, usually completely black or black with some adornment, sometimes completely painted but with a minimum of detail. By contrast, a profile painted in color with shading clearly shows features, skin tones, and clothing. It is more similar to a traditional frontal portrait.

The Use of Stock Bodies

Some artists speeded up the silhouetting process by using printed lithograph bodies that were cut out, painted with water colors, and pasted to the paper on which the profile had been produced (see page 63). Another shortcut was to stamp on a block-printed body (see page 64), though these were much less common.

Sometimes you will hear authorities refer to stock bodies when discussing *painted* portraits. Their theory is that traveling artists carried canvasses with just a body painted on. When commissioned to do a portrait, all they had to do was add the head. I believe that some people have tended to confuse portrait painters with silhouette artists, whose headless stock bodies have been found from time to time. To my knowledge, portrait canvasses without heads have not been discovered.

An Artistic Heritage

Silhouette cutting is part of our artistic heritage. It enjoyed approximately fifty years of popularity until the advent of photography in the 1840s. An art form that was popular for this length of time must be recognized for its contribution to the aesthetic side of this heritage.

The art of the silhouettist is fascinating. It was simple and dignified. It was not easy to capture the likeness and manner of a subject in profile by a few clippings from a simple sheet of paper and a minimum of detail using a few brushstrokes. Yet the best silhouettists accomplished this with great facility.

CHAPTER ONE

The Basics

FEW GOOD BOOKS have been written about American silhouettes
and silhouettists of earlier days. The two best books are probably Alice
Van Leer Carrick's *Shades of Our Ancestors* (1928) and Mrs. E. Nevill
Jackson's *Silhouette: Notes and Dictionary* (1938). Though the
originals went out of print many years ago, Charles E. Tuttle Co.,
publishers, of Rutland, Vermont, reprinted the Carrick book in 1968
under the title *A History of American Silhouettes: A Collector's
Guide*. It has since gone out of print also. In 1981, Dover Publications,
Inc. published an unabridged paperback version of the Jackson work
titled *Silhouettes: A History and Dictionary of Artists*. As of this
writing, this Jackson book is still available.

The Carrick book is quite informative. It discusses a sizable number
of documented silhouette artists, their styles, and various methods of
producing silhouettes. The Jackson book has an American section
and a large listing of known silhouette artists. If you are a collector
looking for good sources of information, I recommend that you
obtain the Carrick and Jackson books—in that order—from your
public library.

About the Period 1790 to 1840

The years covered by this book—from 1790 into the 1840s—are
those of greatest interest to the average collector. This is when the best
work was done. During that fifty-year period, silhouettes were a quick
and economical way to acquire a likeness of oneself or one's family
members as a remembrance. After 1840, photographs became in-
creasingly available, reducing the popularity and demand for
silhouettes.

Silhouetting Methods

There were three major methods for producing silhouettes—
hollow-cutting, cutting and pasting, and painting.

To make a *hollow-cut* silhouette, the artist cut a profile out of the

1

center of a piece of white paper with scissors, leaving no broken line to the edge of the paper. The outline for this type of silhouette was almost always prepared by the use of a mechanical contrivance. One such mechanical aid, a *Pantograph*, consisted of bars that were so adjusted that a steel tracer, equipped with an elbow to allow movement in all directions, rotated around the sitter's head and upper body. This tracer worked in unison with a steel point or lead pencil at the other end of the bar, creating the reduced profile onto paper or card. The artist would then cut out the reduced outline, refining it as he cut, occasionally leaving some of the original marks from the machine on the paper. He then laid the cut profile over a piece of dark paper or fabric such as silk to provide contrast. This paper or fabric background was usually black.

For the *cut-and-pasted* type, the artist fashioned a silhouette from black paper and glued it to a white paper background. Some of these backgrounds had painted or printed exterior or interior scenes. Most of the cut-and-pasted silhouettes were cut freehand.

The *painted* silhouette was just that. It was completely painted, usually in black, with no cut parts whatsoever. The artist added details by using Chinese white, water color, or bronzing. Of the three major American silhouette types, painted silhouettes are the least common.

Occasionally artists using the cut-and-pasted or the painted techniques also used a mechanical contrivance to obtain an accurate outline of the profile.

Preserving Silhouettes

Among the chapters that follow is a fine one on the conservation and preservation of silhouettes written by C. R. Jones, conservator for the New York State Historical Association at Cooperstown. He is an authority on the subject, and I am grateful that he has contributed his expertise.

CHAPTER TWO

How to Recognize
High-Quality Silhouettes

SILHOUETTES ARE A FORM of art. In searching for a fine silhouette, you should look for many of the same criteria that you would in acquiring a good-quality painting. In this chapter we will discuss precisely what those qualities are and how to become familiar with them.

Learn the Artists

To begin, go to museums, exhibits, and silhouette sales. Familiarize yourself with the wide variety of styles and with the different artists in this field. Once you can recognize what museums consider good quality, you will soon be able to make those distinctions for yourself. Next, go to libraries and study books with photographs of work by documented silhouettists. Become familiar with their techniques of cutting and painting. Look for individuality. Most silhouettists had peculiar styles that, with close scrutiny, you can distinguish from the styles of others. Signatures and marks are an additional aid to identification, but it is best not to rely on them—they can easily be faked. In the end, style, quality, and technique really determine who did the work.

Keep in mind that there are many documented silhouettists who were very talented; others were less accomplished. Yet the craftsmanship of any silhouettist, known or unknown, may not be consistent enough to warrant that each piece be included in a private or public collection. It is important to recognize the strength in the piece itself.

Recognizing Quality

No matter who the artist is, it is essential that the silhouette be well cut. The entire outline should have smooth edges, no jagged or rough cuts, and no wiggly lines. Clearly cut silhouettes mark a steady hand, a sure sign of a good artist. The features of the sitter should be well defined. Intricate details, like an eyelash, are especially desirable.

3

The same characteristics of quality apply to painted silhouettes. Smooth edges, well-defined features, and intricacy of detail are all marks of excellence. In addition, painted silhouettes usually have such embellishments as hair, collars, stocks, vests, bonnets, lace, or combs. Some of these items may be painted on in various tones of the same black India ink or water color that comprise the main portion of the silhouette. Sometimes the details are enhanced by the use of Chinese white or an application of gold paint, a technique known as *bronzing*. Whatever the method, these embellishments should show a well-trained hand. A fine silhouette of this type can have artistic merit comparable to a good painting.

Look for the Details

Once you have found a good-quality silhouette, look closely at the fine detail. Hair, for example, should be delineated delicately and built up with many strokes to achieve a realistic look. If the silhouettist's style is more naive, the hair will be more stylized, less delicate.

If bonnets with lace or men's dressy stocks are indicated, they should be executed to show a softness appropriate to the fabric. Here again, in a primitive or "folky" silhouette these details would be less graceful and more simplified.

You can also find embellishments such as these in the hollow-cut and cut-and-pasted varieties, and there you should use the same criteria for evaluation. Occasionally the artist enhanced the clothing by the use of color. It offers a nice relief from the stark black and white, adding further interest and appeal to the silhouette.

In all silhouettes with painted embellishments, the quality of the detail work will vary greatly. Look for a silhouette with most, if not all, of its components done well.

Look for Even Quality

I have seen a pair of silhouettes that at first glance appeared to be charming. They were folky, with hollow-cut faces and India ink wash or water color bodies. The bodies were of fine quality. When I closely examined the faces, however, I noticed rough cutting that was, at best, mediocre. Since silhouettes are meant to be portraits, I found this pair undesirable. Had the faces been well defined and chiseled and the costumes slightly less accomplished, these two silhouettes would have been of higher quality.

Good Condition or Poor?

The condition of the silhouette is important. Staining, tears, and signs of bugs or mold are all undesirable. If the silhouette in poor condition is unique or of high artistic merit by a well-known artist, it may be worth purchasing anyway. This can be a difficult decision. Of course, if you do buy a silhouette in such condition, you should plan on having it restored.

If a silhouette is badly damaged, pass it up. If it has only a few stains that do not touch the figure itself, or if the tears are small and do not cut through the figure except minimally, it could be worth purchasing. But remember—the price should reflect the less-than-optimal condition.

Are the Frame and Glass Original?

If you find a well-executed silhouette in good to fine condition that has a frame original to the piece, you really have something worthwhile. If it has the original glass, which will sometimes be enameled on the reverse in black and ringed or decorated with gold (called *eglomise*), and a signature of the artist or his or her original label, you may have acquired a museum-quality silhouette! This is the ultimate find. I can assure you that there are silhouettes like this out there for those who know what to look for.

CHAPTER THREE

How to Increase Your Chances of Acquiring a Genuine Antique Silhouette

WHEN YOU HAVE DONE your homework, as recommended in the previous chapters, you are already off to a good start in acquiring a fine antique silhouette. If you can recognize the particular style of a silhouette artist and can appreciate artistic and aesthetic workmanship, you have reached your first goal. You will be able to tell immediately whether a silhouette is not of the period, is not by the hand to whom it is attributed, or is not worth owning. This is good, but there is much more to know.

Are They Copies or Fakes?

Early silhouettes were often copied by relatives of the silhouette subjects, so that there would be more likenesses to share with other family members. While these copies are not fakes, it would have been helpful if they had been marked COPY so that they could not possibly be passed on later as originals. Usually the degree of aesthetic and artistic quality of copies was considerably diminished. As you develop a discerning eye, you will be able to recognize silhouette copies as being less well made.

Some silhouettes, of course, *are* intended to deceive. They are fakes, and often very clever ones at that. Recognizing them is extremely difficult. Is the paper old and good? A devious silhouette reproducer may have used a flyleaf from an old book for his cutting. He may have diligently reproduced an artist's style and signature. This is the time you must recall from memory the many original silhouette styles and signatures you have seen. As you examine the piece, ask yourself: Is the quality of execution there?

You should scrutinize a silhouette the way an antique furniture collector would examine a piece of early country furniture predating 1840. He or she would look for the right nails, typical shrinkage (a roundtop table would have gone out of round), signs of hand planing or the pit saw on the underside or back of boards, peg or mortise-and-tenon joinery, and so on. *The point is this: If you recall from memory all the signs of quality plus the signs of age and add them up, the piece must meet these criteria.*

Follow the Paper Trail

Ask yourself, Does the paper look good? Most good dealers will allow you to take a silhouette out of its frame to examine it more closely. Do it. Is the paper "laid," showing a texture of parallel lines? Is it "wove," having a smooth texture? "Wove" paper is the more usual and is safer. If it is "laid," the silhouette is probably earlier than 1810.

Is there a difference in the color of the paper where the frame has been resting? There should be. The paper is usually darker where it has been exposed through the glass and lighter behind the protecting frame. In the hollow-cut silhouette, sometimes an outline of the black paper or cloth behind the open cut is evident as a shape directly behind the face of the subject.

For silhouettes where a wood backing was used behind the frame, the back of the paper from which the silhouette was cut may actually show the grain of the wood upon which it has rested.

Familiarize yourself with the paper used in books printed between 1790 and 1840. Does the paper used for the silhouette have similar properties and appearance? Was ink used for a signature, to identify the sitter, or for a date? Look at the ink color. Age usually will have faded black ink to a brownish or yellowish brown hue.

Marks from the Mechanical Contrivance

From time to time on the hollow-cut variety of silhouette, you can see faint lines around portions of the figure, made from the mechanical contrivance as it reduced the outline of the sitter. They look like stylus marks, and on some occasions these outlines may be in pencil. They won't completely surround the silhouette. These are the marks around the figure that the silhouette artist chose to disregard to refine the outline, thereby achieving a more satisfactory result.

The stylus marks are an especially reassuring factor towards the authenticity of the silhouette. Do not rely on these marks alone, since it is always possible that a forger may have acquired one of these mechanical devices. The odds, however, are with you.

Learn the Costume and Hair Styles

Learn to recognize the dress styles and hair styles of this period. The silhouette must match these styles without any doubt. For instance, men's hair styled long in the back, pulled together and tied with a ribbon or braided, had disappeared by the early 1800s. Thus a silhouette of a man with a shirt collar that sits up high on the cheek—an 1820 or 1830 style—and long hair tied back is one you should definitely disregard. This is an oversimplification, but you see the point.

Years ago, clothing and hair styles overlapped, as they do today. Studying these styles will aid you in spotting any discrepancies. For a further discussion of the clothing and hair styles from 1790 to 1840, see Chapter Four.

Be Aware of Changed Frames

Many silhouettes were not framed at the time they were originally produced. Some owners put them between the pages of a book, in the family Bible, and in an assortment of other places. Later owners may have framed them, and still-later owners framed them yet again. That is why you can find charming silhouettes with paper faded or discolored in various shapes within shapes from the previous framings. It is also why you may find a wonderful early silhouette in an inappropriate Victorian frame. So look beyond the frame. Concentrate on the silhouette itself.

Be Cautious—But Persevere

Do not be discouraged. As you study authentic, high-quality silhouettes, you will gradually gain a feeling and an eye for aesthetic merit, fine craftsmanship, and artistic talent. You will recognize the work of known silhouettists without even looking for their marks or signatures. You will know the signs of age on paper and ink, and you will be able to quickly date a piece by the costume or hair style. *Repetition* of this kind of study is the key to acquiring confidence.

Remember: One sign of quality and one sign of age are not enough. The silhouette must have enough signs of both to satisfy you that it is a high-quality original.

The Wallace Nutting Copies

In 1915, a Wallace Nutting catalogue offered copies of early silhouettes. These were prints, and to an untrained eye they may appear genuine. Usually you will find the Wallace Nutting label on the back, though many have been removed. These silhouettes are printed on shiny paper typical of this period. If you are observant, you will be unlikely to mistake them for originals.

When in Doubt, Pass It Up

One last word. Do not hesitate to pass up a silhouette if you feel unsure about it. If something nags at you that you can't quite put your finger on, let it go. Over years of handling, collecting, and seeing silhouettes, you will develop a sixth sense that is the best test of all. You will find others on the market for your consideration. In the search for antique silhouettes, time and patience are your best guides.

CHAPTER FOUR

Dating Silhouettes
by Costume and Hair Styles

UNLESS THE DATE IS actually inscribed on it, no one can pinpoint an antique to a definite year. We have already discussed many of the indications of age, but that is all they are—indications. They simply give us a framework by which to judge.

When you are trying to date a silhouette by the subject's costume and hair style, usually the best you can do is to assign it to a particular time span. You might conclude, for example, that a given silhouette was cut between 1790 and 1800, or between 1820 and 1825. To give a more specific date might be impossible. That is because fashions overlapped—older styles were often worn for a time after newer styles had already appeared. For this reason, you will notice that the following descriptions of clothing and hair styles, and the illustrations for them, each cover about ten years. They primarily emphasize changes during that time.

You will also notice that women's hair styles and fashions changed more rapidly than men's did, and that women's clothing styles varied more than men's over the same time span. This is not unlike what we experience today.

Dating by the Details

Because a typical silhouette profile is dark, usually bust length, and shows a minimum of detail, we are given little by which to determine the age of the piece. We are forced to reach a conclusion based on the details the silhouettist included—hair styles, collars, bonnets, shirt frills, cravats, and other small touches.

Full Length vs. Bust Length

There were so many more bust-sized silhouettes produced than full-length ones that the following illustrations will show only the smaller size. The strongest factors for determining age are found in the upper portions of the figures, so it is just as easy to date a full-length silhouette from these same details.

1790 TO EARLY 1800S

From 1790 to the early 1800s, men wore military-style coats with stand-up collars for casual occasions and coats with high necks and no collars for more formal events. In both instances, the shirt had a frilly front and a band, usually white, was draped around the neck and tied into a small knot below the chin. A front-buttoned vest was worn over the shirt.

Men wore their hair long, often tied in back with a ribbon, and they sometimes wore a rolled curl above or over each ear.

[1] [2]

Women wore kerchiefs over their shoulders, crossed them in front, and fastened them in back. Wearing several kerchiefs was very fashionable, and the outermost kerchief often had a ruffle at the neckline [4].

At this time American women imitated French women in wearing dresses with low-necked bodices. To prevent the bosom from showing, the kerchiefs were carefully arranged and tucked into the bodice [3]. Bodices were also becoming fuller in the new Empire style, which raised the waistline towards the bust.

The hair was sometimes worn in a short frizzy style in front, with little curls around the face, and pulled up in back, making the entire hair-do look short [3]. At other times, women curled the hair with a hot curling iron, powdered it, and piled it high on top of the head with soft, long curls at the neckline. Also fashionable was a large bonnet, pulled together in the middle with a satin ribbon to make a fluffy top.

[3]   [4]

The neckline of a little girl's dress was wide, low cut, and decorated with narrow lace. Her hair fell long and wavy to the shoulders, and her bangs were straight.

A boy wore a coat with a plain vest and a blouse. A kerchief similar to a woman's or the wide lacy collar of his blouse covered the top of both the vest and coat. His hair was cut in a short pageboy style, with bangs covering the forehead.

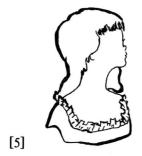 

[5]   [6]

1800 TO 1810

After 1800, men's coats had high-standing collars and lapels that folded back. Striped as well as plain vests were worn and the cravat was wrapped around the neck in such a manner that it came up onto the chin. The ends were lapped over each other and tucked into the vest [8]. Cravats were also worn in the more traditional manner—wrapped

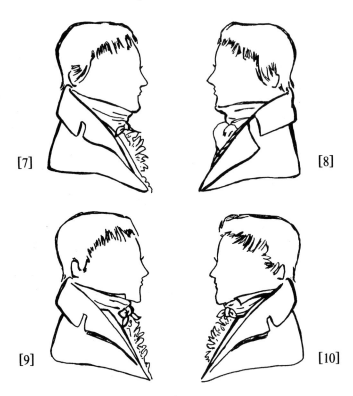

[7]   [8]

[9]   [10]

around the neck and tied in front with a small knot [7]. Occasionally a small collar appeared above the cravat [9] or slightly over the cravat [10].

Men's hair was worn short and brushed toward the face.

Women's fashions and hair styles became quite varied during this decade. The traditional low-cut bodice, filled in discreetly with a kerchief, and the mop cap were still evident [11], but many new styles had begun to appear.

With the invention of the cotton gin at the end of the 1700s, cotton cloth became more readily available. Such soft material opened the way for styles with Greek and Roman influence. The high waistline was under the bosom, and the material covering the bust was softly shirred. The neckline was low and filled in with a delicately embroidered cloth and a neck cloth called a *ruff*. The hairdo was often Grecian in style with ribbons winding around curls that had been oiled [12].

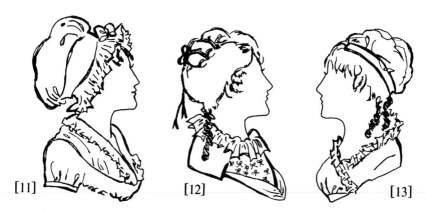

[11]   [12]   [13]

A full, high-waisted dress—an early Empire style—had developed also. Sometimes a kerchief was tucked into the neckline of the full front. At other times, the front had two pieces of fabric; one crossed over the other and fastened with a hook and eye [13]. A ribbon wrapped around the hair, which had been curled with a hot curling iron, also reflected the Empire style.

[14]   [15]

Little girls wore soft muslin dresses with drawstrings around the neckline, in the middle of the bodice, and around the waist. Girls' hair was very short and was brushed toward the face.

Little boys wore double-breasted suits and jackets and frilly blouses. Their hair was cut short with bangs. Younger boys wore their hair in a long pageboy, again with bangs.

1810 TO 1820S

During this period particularly, styles overlapped. The drawings that follow are few, but they show the most important changes between the early 1800s and the 1830s.

Men's coats were double and single breasted with high collars. The coat shoulders were wide, with the sleeves full and gathered at the shoulder, gradually becoming narrower as they approached the wrists and flared out over the hands.

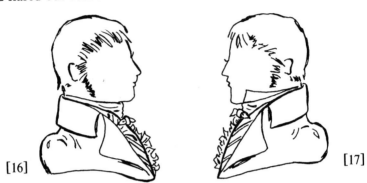

[16]   [17]

The shirt once again had a frilled front that showed under a vest with lapels. The tie was knotted in front [16]. On occasion, the shirt collar showed open and high above the cravat. This was to be the usual in the next two decades [17].

The hair style was short and brushed toward the face, with long sideburns running down the cheeks.

Women's dress bodices were still gathered to a certain degree at this time. The necklines remained low and the sleeves worn either long or short. When short, the sleeve was flared at the lower section instead of

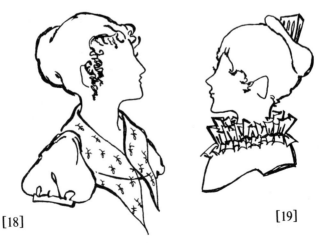

[18]   [19]

at the shoulder and had a tight band where the sleeve ended. Printed kerchiefs worn around the neck were very popular. Ruffs were worn at the neck, a style that continued into the 1830s.

The hair was still worn piled up in back, though with more curls and a few ringlets around the face. Combs were often worn.

[20]   [21]

Little girls wore high-waisted dresses with bodices much less full than their mothers'. The hair was long, braided, and wrapped around the head with ribbons on top.

Little boys' outfits had slightly high waists and their jackets had lapels. They wore blouses with wide collars that were trimmed with lace. The hair length varied.

1820 TO 1830

Men's coat collars in the 1820s were high in back but lower in front, with a more rounded look to the collar and lapels, which were sewn together where the bottom of the collar met the top of the lapel. Men's coats were often double breasted and were usually worn open. The sleeves were slightly less full at the shoulder, yet remained narrow at the wrist and continued to flare out over the hand right into the 1830s.

During this period, the shirt collar often showed above the cravat or tie. The collar stood up against the cheeks, while the tie—either white or black—still wrapped around the neck and tied in a knot in front [23]. The shirts by this time had tucked fronts, though you will occasionally find a frilly front. The frill was most often a single, worn only on one side of the shirt opening. The vests were primarily striped [22].

Top hats became popular at this time. Men started to part their hair and wore the top forward yet puffier and higher. A more curly look was common, with long sideburns [23].

[22]   [23]

Women's dresses in the 1820s still had the high waist of the Empire style. The low necklines were no longer filled in with kerchiefs. Instead, women wore a ruff—a pleated, round, heavily starched collar popular in the sixteenth century [25]. They also wore standard collars [24]. At this time, sleeves were slowly growing larger and puffier at the top.

Hair was still piled on top of the head, though broken up by a comb at the back. Ringlets were still worn over the face and often rolled curls over the ears. Also, bonnets were becoming popular once again.

[24]   [25]

Little girls' dresses remained similar to the previous decade, except that the sleeves were becoming fuller. Girls' hair was worn either short and brushed onto the face or parted in the center with a tiny bang and bunches of curls high over the ears.

[26]   [27]

Young boys' clothes were more adult looking, often a double-breasted coat worn with a striped vest. The shirt might have a wide, stand-away folded collar. Boys' hair was short and combed forward.

1830 TO 1840

By the 1830s, men's coats were almost always double breasted and tight fitting. The lapels had notches where they met the collar. These notches appeared in earlier years and lasted into the 1840s, but most coats with this detailing were worn in the 1830s.

[28]   [29]

The cravat was tied in a bow [28] rather than a knot. Sometimes it was just wrapped around the neck, giving the appearance of a band [29]. The cravat might be black or white.

Hair was worn both curly and straight, frequently with sideburns.

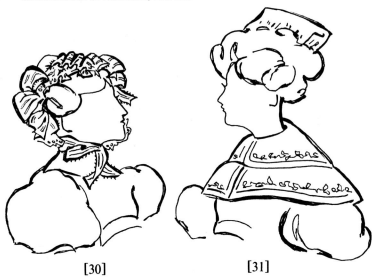

[30]   [31]

Women's dresses in the early 1830s had waistlines slightly higher than the natural waistline. The neckline was very wide and sometimes went off and down the shoulders [30]. Sleeves were very full and puffy above the elbow. Some were so enormous that they had to be stuffed to achieve the proper look. Wide belts were worn and eventually the waistline returned to its natural position. Dress collars became quite large and, because of their width, fell over the sleeves [31].

The hair was usually parted in the middle of the front, then combed down and back or curled at the sides in large rolls [30]. The back was worn in a bun, piled on top of the head in a top knot, or drawn up and wound around a wide comb [31]. Ruffled, lacy, sheer bonnets were very popular [30].

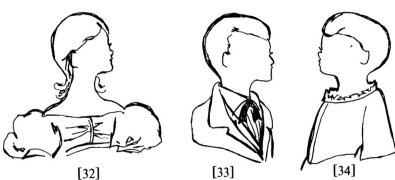

[32]   [33]   [34]

Girls wore dresses with the wide neckline that went below the shoulders. The sleeves were quite full and were sometimes filled with small pillows stuffed with feathers to give them this huge look. The bodices were tucked and sometimes aprons were worn.

Girls' hair was often parted in the center and worn pulled back behind the ears.

Boys wore short jackets. Their clothes were quite elegant—they often wore a vest with lapels and a black cravat—and their hair was combed in a side part.

Younger boys wore tunics and smocks. The tunic was worn with a chemise underneath that showed a ruffle at the neck and long sleeves where the tunic sleeve ended. The smock had a neckline that ran off the shoulder. Little boys also wore pantalets that, along with the skirt of the dress, were shorter than the ones worn by little girls. They also wore their hair in the new side part.

By keeping a sharp eye on these costume and hair styles as they evolved during this fifty-year period, you can develop an ability to assign an antique silhouette to the period in which it was cut. This is a satisfying skill to develop and, for the serious collector, an essential one.

CHAPTER FIVE

Photographs of Silhouettes from Private Collections

Documented Silhouettists

24

No. 1
HOLLOW-CUT SILHOUETTE BY WM. KING

1804-1809

AUTHOR'S COLLECTION

Here is a silhouette in its simplest form. It is hollow cut with no adornment, yet King achieved a certain charm and sophistication in such simplicity. This is an accomplishment not to be taken lightly. As stated in the main text of the book, "It was not easy to capture the likeness and manner of a subject in profile by a few clippings from a simple sheet of paper." King was a master at this.

I found this piece at an outdoor show placed in the original brass frame, wrong side out. There was powder on the surrounding paper, evidently put there to lighten the darkness formed by the normal aging process. The quality and manner of cutting immediately brought Wm. King's name to mind and at the shoulder line I noticed a few bumps. Could this be the back of his embossed signature? The dealer agreed to my removing the silhouette from the frame, and when I turned it over the embossed Wm. King signature was there. I was ecstatic over my find! Unfortunately the signature does not show up in the photograph.

The opportunity arises again to advise removing the silhouette from its frame whenever possible, and that *repeated* studying of the silhouette artists' work, their styles, and their techniques is paramount.

No. 2
HOLLOW-CUT SILHOUETTE BY WM. DOYLE
ca. 1810
AUTHOR'S COLLECTION

This is a delicately executed silhouette by a very early silhouette artist who came from Boston and probably always worked there. The frill of the shirt is somewhat stylized, which is typical of Doyle. The hair is rather wispy. Also typical is the shape of cutting he uses at the lower left portion of the profile. His printed signature is delicate yet extremely clear and neat.

The black paper over which the open cut of the silhouette is laid has a sheen to it and can be classified as *flint* paper, a paper of the period but not commonly found.

Notice the inappropriate Victorian frame. This is the way I acquired it, and I chose to leave it in this frame because it is difficult to find a period frame to fit both the silhouette and what appears to be the silhouette's original eglomise mat. Remember, never cut down the original size of the silhouette to fit a frame. The less you tamper with the original, the more an antique will hold its value.

No. 3
HOLLOW-CUT SILHOUETTE BY WM. DOYLE

ca. 1810
AUTHOR'S COLLECTION

This is the same Doyle silhouette out of its frame. Notice the fine tears in the white paper in four locations on the silhouette. These did not do any damage to the profile itself. Therefore, I had them stabilized by C. R. Jones through a restoration process that prevents them from tearing anymore. The paper was spray-wetted and mended from behind with Japanese tissue and rice starch paste.

This silhouette I found in a frame that was not original and it also needed some obvious restoration. I decided to purchase it because it was executed by an important silhouettist whose work I like. I felt that the tears, once restored, were not threatening to the portrait.

No. 4
HOLLOW-CUT SILHOUETTE ATTRIBUTED TO WM. CHAMBERLAIN

1820s

PRIVATE COLLECTION

New Hampshire resident Caleb Cross's silhouette is well cut in its somewhat folky style. Notice the proportion of the head is exaggerated in comparison to the smaller body. The treatment of the cravat and vest is rather stylized. There are two hollow-cut areas—the head and the portion of the body below the lapels. It is a little difficult to see the full shape of the lapels, as they have been painted black and lay over the silhouette paper, which is black also.

The simple gold frame with its eglomise mat appears to be original to the profile. Notice at the top of the portrait that the paper has slipped downward a little, showing the lighter color of the paper that had been protected by the frame. Remember, this tends to lend credence to age. If you were to see the actual silhouette, you would notice at that point faint scallops that match the scalloping on the glass. These indicate that the mat is original to the silhouette.

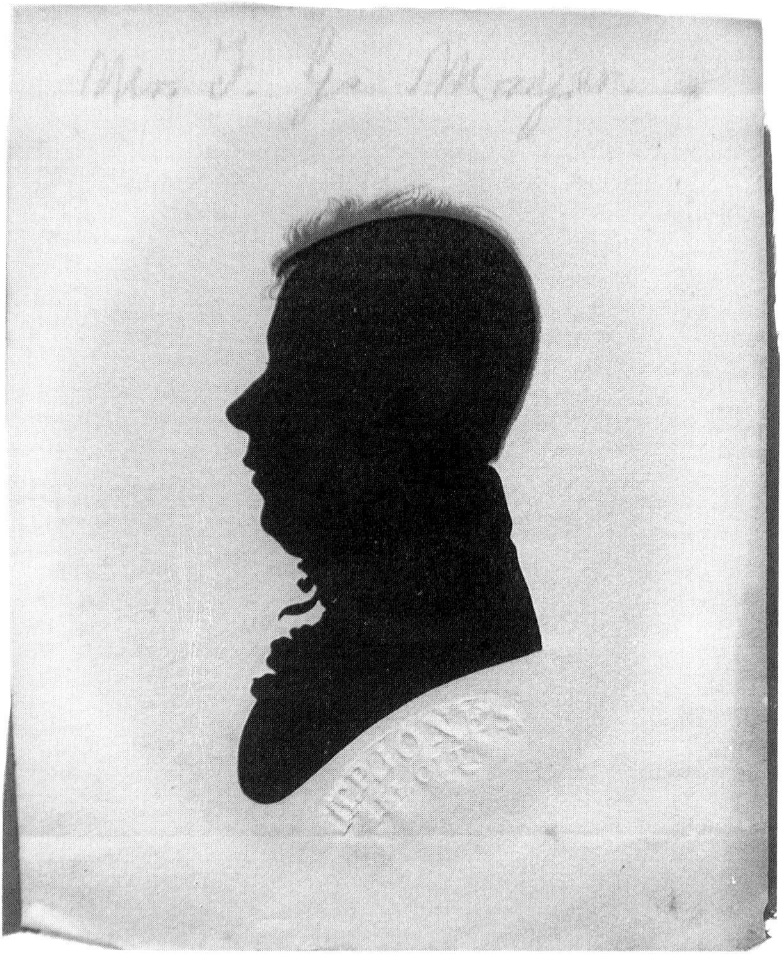

No. 5
HOLLOW-CUT SILHOUETTE BY T. P. JONES

ca. 1810

PRIVATE COLLECTION

This is a finely executed silhouette, very precise in the details of the frilled shirt front and tie. The cutting is laid over black silk. The hair is delicately delineated.

Notice the darker color of the paper shaped as an oval where the silhouette is exposed through the frame, and the lighter shade of the paper where the frame has been resting. This color change helps to establish that the silhouette is old and is probably in its original frame, since the frame has an oval opening matching the oval on the paper.

Take note of the embossed signature: *T. P. Jones—Fecit.*

The writing at the top in pencil is most likely the name of the subject. It looks like *T. G. Mayer.*

No. 6
HOLLOW-CUT SILHOUETTE BY T. P. JONES

ca. 1810

PRIVATE COLLECTION

Here is the same Jones silhouette in what appears to be its original stamped brass frame. The embossed signature is a little harder to see now, and the writing at the top is almost completely covered up.

This is another good reason to take a silhouette out of its frame for examination before purchasing. One never knows when some pertinent information such as a date, name, or locality may be written in some concealed area.

No. 7
HOLLOW-CUT SILHOUETTE BY PEALE
1790–1800
AUTHOR'S COLLECTION

This silhouette from Rome, New York, has well-defined features and the stamp *Museum* embossed under the bustline. The stamp is very faint so it does not show up in the photograph. This is one of the known signatures of the Peale artists, most likely Charles Wilson Peale, who had a museum located in Independence Hall in Philadelphia, Pa.

The silhouette is special because it is so early. Notice the hairdo, worn long and tied with a bow in back. Few silhouettes are found from this period.

No. 8
HOLLOW-CUT SILHOUETTE BY J. A. DAVIS
Dated October 20, 1832
COLLECTION OF LEWIS W. SCRANTON

J. A. Davis has always been known for his water color portraits until this silhouette appeared. His water colors are represented in some of the finest folk art museums and private collections throughout the country.

This collector had the silhouette authenticated at the Abby Aldrich Rockefeller Folk Art Center in Colonial Williamsburg, Va. Reference is made to the profile on page 80 in *American Folk Portraits, Paintings and Drawings from the Abby Aldrich Rockefeller Folk Art Center*, Beatrix T. Rumford, general editor.

The features are well chiseled, the water color body is stylized, and the signature is quite bold. Because of its rarity, it would be a prize for any collector or museum.

Nos. 9 & 10
PAIR OF HOLLOW-CUT SILHOUETTES BY WM. BACHE

ca. 1810

PRIVATE COLLECTION

William Bache began his career in Philadelphia, Pennsylvania, and then traveled extensively. In my opinion, he was one of the finest silhouette artists. As you'll notice in these two excellent examples of unknown sitters, the detail work has the esthetics and painterly quality of an

accomplished artist. The man's hair and some of the woman's lace are delicately painted in black and the details of both the man's and woman's clothing are well executed in Chinese white on the silhouette paper. This method of painting directly on the black background paper of a hollow-cut silhouette is quite unusual among the American silhouette artists.

The profiles are well chiseled and the total effect is outstanding.

Notice Bache's embossed signature. It is an oval with *Bache's* at the top and *Patent* at the bottom with little rosettes in the center.

41

No. 11
COMPLETELY PAINTED SILHOUETTE BY MOSES CHAPMAN

Early 1800s

PRIVATE COLLECTION

This painted silhouette is very detailed. Careful attention has been paid to the hair and to the lace at the top of the dress bodice. The comb has a translucent quality that is difficult to achieve.

Although there is a slight water stain at the lower right portion of the paper, it would not prevent me from purchasing the profile.

This portrait was originally in the collection of the Rev. Glenn Tilley Morse of West Newbury, Mass., who I understand was a highly regarded early collector of silhouettes.

No. 12
PAINTED SILHOUETTE BY WM. BACHE
SUBJECT: WILLIAM BROWN MARTIN, ESQ.,
OF NEWBURYPORT, MASS.

1790–1800
AUTHOR'S COLLECTION

It is not often that one acquires a completely painted silhouette. As mentioned in the text, the most common were the hollow-cut and cut-and-pasted varieties.

This silhouette is not only of a handsome man, but is handsomely executed. Notice the wonderful hair detail, so delicate, and the braid with its bow.

The cravat and the coat details are very clear. The one exception to the fine execution of detail is that the shirt frill is painted in Chinese white, making the part that is next to the white paper barely perceptible. That is acceptable because everything else is so fine. Also notice a portion of Bache's written signature at the bottom right. Over the years much of it has faded.

No. 13
HOLLOW-CUT SILHOUETTE BY WM. BACHE

Early 1800s

COLLECTION OF LEWIS W. SCRANTON

Portraits of charming young girls are always appealing. They seem to exude an innocence that Bache has captured expertly in this profile. The shape of her head is perfection and the delicate wisps of hair hanging off her forehead add just the right touch.

The Chinese white detailing on the low curved neckline of her dress is what is needed to prevent the profile from being too stark.

She appears poised and confident but not overly so. This silhouette shows a true artist at work.

Crist without Heads by W J J Honeywell

No. 14
CUT-AND-PASTED SILHOUETTE BY M.A. HONEYWELL

ca. 1800s

PRIVATE COLLECTION

Upon first glance, one might not be impressed by this profile. It is very impressive, however, because it was cut with a scissors held in the mouth of a woman who had no hands, stumps for arms, and only one foot with three toes.

Notice how smooth the cutting is. There are no jagged or rough cuts. She even wrote at the bottom, "Cut without hands by M.A. Honeywell."

Her accomplishments were amazing and many. She did fine needlework and penmanship as well as cutting profiles. A representative piece of her work would be significant to any collection, public or private.

Nos. 15 & 16
PAIR OF HOLLOW-CUT SILHOUETTES ATTRIBUTED
TO WM. CHAMBERLAIN

1820s

PRIVATE COLLECTION

William Chamberlain's talent is very apparent in these two examples of extremely well-cut and detailed silhouettes. Notice how finely carved the features are. The detailing is done with a gray wash and is meticulously executed.

The woman's collar, known as a *ruff*, has very fine lines forming a

pattern of triangles where the ruff meets the top of the dress. In the photograph these series of lines forming each triangle tend to run together, making the triangles look more solid than they actually are.

Just above the base of the silhouette you can see the belt indication on either side of her torso. How subtle it is!

The man is wearing the popular striped vest and the ruffle that is attached to only one side of the shirt. Just below the collar and lapel of his coat is another hollow-cut area.

These silhouettes appear to be in their original stamped brass frames. This certainly adds to their appeal and value. I would give them museum-quality status.

No. 17
PAINTED SILHOUETTE BY GEORGE CATLIN
Dated 1824
PRIVATE COLLECTION

Mr. Fred H. Robertson must have been pleased with this portrait by George Catlin. The profile is very well defined and many pains have been taken to give the hair a soft, realistic appearance.

The proportions are excellent and a fine painterly quality is evident throughout. This is a good example of what I mentioned in Chapter 2: A fine silhouette of this type can have artistic merit comparable to a good painting.

George Catlin was a self-taught painter who went west in the 1830s and painted Indians and Indian life. Much of his work is in Washington, D. C.

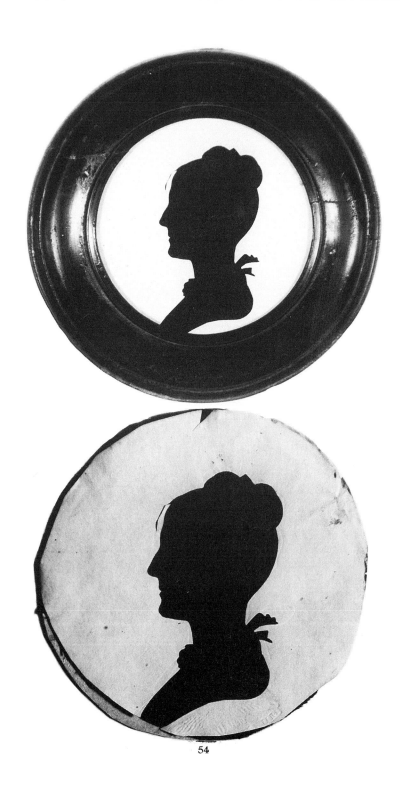

Nos. 18 & 19
HOLLOW-CUT SILHOUETTE BY PEALE

Early 1800s
AUTHOR'S COLLECTION

This is a profile that has one of the Peale embossed signatures under the bust curve. It is an eagle with its wings spread and under that is printed *Peale's Museum.*

I was attracted to the silhouette at an antique show because it resembled a Peale. Upon looking it over, I found the shape of the eagle barely discernable, as it was so low in the frame. Not being able to take it apart did not, however, deter me from purchasing it.

Closer inspection at home verified my attribution, but I was dismayed that someone had cut a portion of the bottom away, evidently to make it fit the frame. As you can see, the paper has an open cut at the left bust line. The only remains of the signature are a portion of the eagle and the *um* from *Museum.* None of it should have been tampered with. If someone were intent on reducing the size, he should have removed part of the top where nothing would have been lost!

This is an *excellent* example of how important it is, whenever possible, to examine a silhouette out of its frame before purchasing it. Had I known the condition before buying it, I might have taken it anyway. It is a good example of a Peale woman and the price was far below what a perfect one would have cost.

Look very closely at the profile out of the frame. Around the hairline at the back of her head and around the tie at the back of her neck, you should be able to see the faint lines from the mechanical contrivance before the profile was refined.

No. 20
COMPLETELY PAINTED SILHOUETTE BY WM. BACHE
ca. 1815
PRIVATE COLLECTION

Jane Strawbridge Ledyard's silhouette is an exquisite all-painted profile of a beautiful woman from a prominent Cazenovia, New York, family. The profile is very well defined and her hair is delicately rendered. There is a slight indication of a comb at the back portion of the top of her head.

The ruff around her neck looks soft and fluffy with its black washes and touches of Chinese white. The white may be a little hard to see. The papier-mache frame is original and the silhouette is in excellent condition.

It is a handsome silhouette, done in the least common of the three major American silhouette methods by one of our finest silhouette artists. Bache's additions to the basic profile almost always have a sensitive painterly quality. This is a silhouette any musem would be pleased to own.

Unidentified Silhouettists

No. 21
HOLLOW-CUT SILHOUETTE OF A CHILD
Early 1800s
PRIVATE COLLECTION

Silhouettes of children, especially young ones, are uncommon. This is a charming little girl, probably no older than three or four.

She is very well cut. There is a strong indication achieved by the pure talent of the silhouette artist that this child has chunky cheeks. Notice the puffiness under the chin. Wouldn't chubby cheeks naturally follow? This aspect of the silhouette provides a fine example of how a talented artist can provide much information with the least amount of detail.

Her hair and the lace above the neckline of her dress are fine added touches. The stamped brass frame is probably the original.

Nos. 22 & 23

HOLLOW-CUT SILHOUETTES

1830s

AUTHOR'S COLLECTION

Here are two very-well-cut silhouettes of Anne and Zeruiah Brodrick, sisters from Massachusetts. At first glance they look much alike. Upon closer scrutiny their differences become more apparent.

The lithograph bodies are an amusing addition to the hollow-cut

Miss Zeruiah Brodrick

silhouette. Lithograph bodies were printed in black and white. The silhouette artist cut them off of the original paper that they were printed on and pasted them to his or her profiles, painting the clothing in various shades for extra interest.

A silhouette similar to these can be found in figure 266 on page 266 of *American Folk Portraits, Paintings and Drawings from the Abby Aldrich Rockefeller Folk Art Center*, Beatrix T. Rumford, general editor.

This silhouette type affords yet another dimension to one's collection.

No. 24
HOLLOW-CUT SILHOUETTE
1820–1830
AUTHOR'S COLLECTION

Here is a well-cut silhouette of a woman with well-defined features. It is obvious she is wearing a comb in her hair, which was a very popular item to include in the hair styles of this period.

What makes this silhouette different—and one a collector should take pleasure in owning—is the block print body stamped onto the paper. Lithograph bodies are unusual, but the block-printed ones are even less common. On page 246 of *American Folk Portraits, Paintings and Drawings from the Abby Aldrich Rockefeller Folk Art Center*, there are photographs of a woman and a man with such bodies.

You will notice in this photograph that some foxing appears around the face and head. This is slight and can either be left alone or restored by a good paper conservator. The silhouette is otherwise in fine condition.

Even with the foxing the silhouette is very worthwhile owning. It is well executed and unusual with the use of a woodblock to print the body, making it possibly appealing for a museum to acquire.

Nos. 25 & 26
PAIR OF HOLLOW-CUT SILHOUETTES
Dated 1810
PRIVATE COLLECTION

The silhouettes of John James and his wife had once been separated; by pure chance they were reunited, to the delight of this private collector. James was a merchant in Manlius, New York, in 1805. He died in 1813 at the age of 28. His wife died in 1858.

These are well-defined, hollow-cut silhouettes with delicate hair detailing. An unusual feature with the original frames is the embossed paper mats in shades of green and white. The mats set the silhouettes off rather nicely.

The owner lives in Manlius, a suburb of Syracuse, New York. It's always exciting to find silhouettes of people from one's own community. Somehow it makes them that much more meaningful.

No. 27
HOLLOW-CUT SILHOUETTE
1830–1840
PRIVATE COLLECTION

This is a wonderful semifolky silhouette of a woman wearing a dress with the typical puffy sleeve of the period. The clothing is executed in an ink or black water color wash. The collar treatment and the ribbon around her neck tied into a bow in front are nice additions. The silhouette artist obviously had a good eye for detail.

The profile is well cut and has a very pleasing expression. The hair and comb are simply defined. This choice of technique works well with the whole. It is a very successful portrait.

The glass mat consists of reverse painting. I believe the glass and the frame are original to the piece.

Nos. 28 & 29
PAIR OF HOLLOW-CUT SILHOUETTES

1820s

PRIVATE COLLECTION

An unusual aspect of these silhouettes is that your eyes seem to focus initially on the lower portion of the profiles before reaching their faces. This can be attributed to the bold treatment along the bust curves. It is

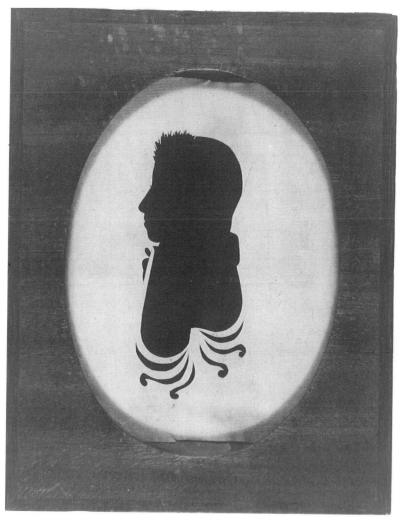

most unique and whimsical and offers an interesting contrast to the conventional cutting of the faces themselves.

The combination of styles is refreshing and successful. This pair exemplifies the innumerable possibilities of styles and techniques used by these imaginative and talented silhouette artists.

No. 30
HOLLOW-CUT SILHOUETTE
1830–1840
PRIVATE COLLECTION

The large stark black profile of this woman offers quite a contrast with the folky body executed delicately and with fine detail. The original pressed brass frame finishes this silhouette off very successfully.

The paper has darkened considerably around the perimeter of the oval but is not undesirable enough to pass up the portrait, for it is quite appealing.

Nos. 31 & 32
PAIR OF HOLLOW-CUT SILHOUETTES
Dated July 1st, 1835
PRIVATE COLLECTION

There must be great pride in owning this very special pair of hollow-cut silhouettes with remarkably stylized bodies. The lower portion of the bodies are hollow-cut but nowhere near as conservatively cut as the faces.

The ink or black water color wash details of the clothing are uniquely executed and the cut-out bustline forms are decorative and exciting.

Sarah and Alanson Gunn, the subjects of these profiles, helped found the town of East Bloomfield, New York, just outside Rochester, in about 1789. They are believed to have originally come from Connecticut.

Silhouettes of this quality in their original frames, with the sitters' names and ages included as well as the date the silhouettes were taken, are highly valued. Include the history connected with them and you've acquired museum-quality pieces.

Nos. 33, 34, 35 & 36
HOLLOW-CUT SILHOUETTES OF THE LOVELL FAMILY
FROM LEOMINSTER, MASS.

Dated 1821

PRIVATE COLLECTION

It doesn't happen very often that one is fortunate enough to acquire silhouettes of an entire family. These four silhouettes of the Lovell family have remained together for more than 160 years.

Well cut by a steady hand and laid over black silk, these silhouettes are in their original frames with the original glass.

A wonderful bonus is that the names of the subjects and their ages are
written at the base of the silhouettes, including the date the profiles were
taken. Some of this writing may not clearly show in the photographs, as it
has faded considerably over the years. Yet in person most of it is quite
legible.

Notice the deviation on the father where certain clothing details were
added in pencil. The writing used to identify him appears to be different
from the writing on the other three. I believe they were all cut by the same
silhouettist, but the father may have written his own name.

Daniel Level Algonquian, R.
1821

No. 37
HOLLOW-CUT SILHOUETTE
1820s
PRIVATE COLLECTION

Modest profiles such as this woman's from New York State can be very appealing. Her small double chin tells us a little more about her. It gives us a chance to play with our imaginations and wonder if she could have been slightly on the plump side.

Her hair is superbly executed and the lace going up her neck and around her neckline is a nice touch.

There are a few cracks in what appears to be the original frame but they have been well mended. It is certainly worth buying.

Nos. 38 & 39
PAIR OF HOLLOW-CUT SILHOUETTES

1830s

AUTHOR'S COLLECTION

Abigail Jumper Sturtevant and Curtis Sturtevant from Dexter, Maine, are the subjects of this pair of hollow-cut silhouettes with water color bodies. They are somewhat folky, especially the man. His body has a special flair to it with its very interesting curved forms.

The hair is less controlled on the man than on the woman. Her comb is well defined and she is wearing eyeglasses. One doesn't often find glasses included on a silhouette.

The woman's dress is a blue gray with a blue ribbon under her lacy ruff, which has a slight repair.

The man's coat is black and he is wearing a blue striped vest, a brown cravat, and a red stickpin. Some of these details are hard to see in a black-and-white photograph, for the colored areas that have the same tonal value tend to blend together.

The black paper behind the hollow-cut heads is flint paper, as in the Doyle silhouette in the previous section. The walnut frames are original. These are fine silhouettes in very good condition that any collector would be proud to own. The faces are well cut, the bodies are well executed, and they have extra interest because they are painted in water color. They are a pair in their original frames, and we know who the sitters are and where they came from.

No. 40
HOLLOW-CUT SILHOUETTE
1830s
AUTHOR'S COLLECTION

This silhouette with a folky painted body came from Montpelier, Vt. There is excellent detailing around the neckline that shows the sitter's jewelry.

The dress is in wonderful shades of light-to-rich medium reds with black striping. She is wearing a well-defined comb in her hair.

The original gold leaf frame has a three-dimensional rope design around the center perimeter. The original glass is decorated with gold-and-black reverse painting.

The woman's features are very clear. She's quite plain looking but portraiture of any kind is meant to create a likeness. These differences help make a collection of portraits more interesting. Considering everything, it is a nice silhouette to own.

No. 41
HOLLOW-CUT SILHOUETTE
ca. 1830
PRIVATE COLLECTION

The confident air of this gentleman is striking with the folky quality of the painted body. The shape of his cravat at the front neckline even adds to his bearing. The vest is a soft yellow; everything else is in shades of black and gray.

He is in good condition except for the light streaks across his arm and chest, where at one time the paper must have been slightly creased. He is a keeper, but the price should reflect his less-than-perfect condition.

Nos. 42 & 43
PAIR OF HOLLOW-CUT SILHOUETTES
1820-1830
PRIVATE COLLECTION

What wonderful folky silhouettes with painted bodies! They are so out of proportion, yet everything works well together to make very pleasing portraits that are fun to look at and to study.

There is good attention paid to detail, including a nice, lightly shaded

area on the man's coat to the left of his sleeve that helps give the silhouette more dimension. A most unusual element is that everything is rendered in black, gray and white—but the hands are painted blue! I have heard some people refer to this profilist as the blue hand silhouettist. No one seems to know any more. In any event, the hands certainly make these portraits unique and more desirable.

These profiles are in their original oval brass frames. The man is in fine condition, but the woman has some of the paper damaged slightly around her chin and especially at the area of the eyelash and forehead.

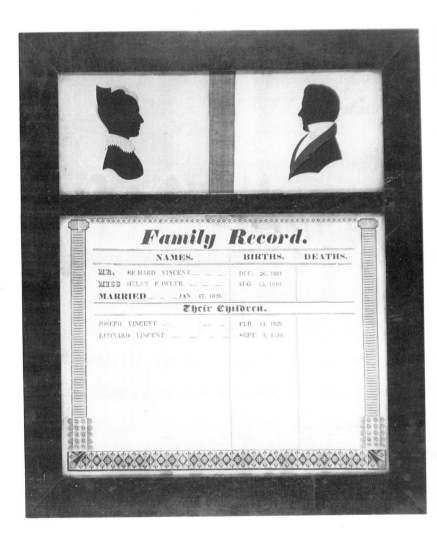

Family Record.

NAMES.	BIRTHS.	DEATHS.
MR. RICHARD VINCENT _ _ _	DEC. 26, 1801	
MISS HELEN FOWLER _ _ _	AUG. 13, 1810	
MARRIED _ _ _JAN. 17, 1828.		

Their Children.

JOSEPH VINCENT _ _ _ _	FEB. 13, 1829.	
LEONARD VINCENT _ _ _ _	SEPT. 7, 1830.	

No. 44
FAMILY RECORD WITH TWO HOLLOW-CUT SILHOUETTES
ca. 1830
PRIVATE COLLECTION

The Richard Vincent family record is a most unusual piece. I have only seen four of these and all appeared to have been done by the same silhouette artist.

This type of family record is illustrated in Alice Van Leer Carrick's book opposite page 136. The New York State Historical Association at Cooperstown owns one with three silhouettes at the top. In each case a green ribbon separates the individual profiles.

What an achievement it would be to find one for one's personal collection! This record is definitely worthy of any museum.

No. 45
HOLLOW-CUT SILHOUETTE
1830-1835
PRIVATE COLLECTION

This is a marvelous silhouette because of its folk art body. The profile is cut by a steady hand, but the features are not as chiseled as they could be.

The painted body in shades of black and gray, with hands included, makes this silhouette extremely desirable. It is not very often that a half-length silhouette is found and with such attention to detail as we see in this vest and coat.

The Abby Aldrich Rockefeller Folk Art Center at Colonial Williamsburg in Virginia owns a pair of silhouettes by this same artist. One can find their photographs in the center's book, *American Folk Portraits* (Beatrix T. Rumford, general editor), on page 257. The text reads, "At least four other half-length profiles have been attributed to the artist responsible for this pair, but only one of them represents the same combination of painting and hollow-cutting seen here. The other three are fully painted side views that do not incorporate cut shapes."

Here is an example of a silhouette that was available to a private collector at an affordable price that is museum quality.

Full-Length Silhouettes

No. 46
FULL-LENGTH, CUT-AND-PASTED SILHOUETTE
SIGNED AUGUSTIN EDOUART

Dated 1842

PRIVATE COLLECTION

Augustin Edouart worked in America from 1839 to 1849. His full-length profiles are highly regarded and prized. This dapper man from Boston may have had a trade connected with the sea in some way. Edouart had numerous lithograph backgrounds against which to display his subjects. The background usually had a connection with their profession or occupation.

Notice the subtlety of the buttons on his coat or vest, the well-defined profile, and the tie around his neck that is blowing in the wind coming off the water. This silhouette and others that are comparable are enjoyed by both private collectors and museums.

No. 47
FULL-LENGTH, CUT-AND-PASTED SILHOUETTE
FOUND NEAR BUFFALO, N.Y.

1830–1840

PRIVATE COLLECTION

This cut-and-pasted silhouette of a man and woman appears to be in the original frame. They are very confidently cut.

There is a modest amount of detail painted on the figures in gold, known as bronzing. The woman's hat and coat cuff are extremely well painted, as are both the figures' shoes and the man's hair. A gray wash indicating grass and shadows is added at the bottom for interest.

No. 48
CUT-AND-PASTED SILHOUETTE BY ALLISON OF NEWBURG
Dated 1841
PRIVATE COLLECTION

Schuyler Hamilton, a West Point cadet, is the subject of this full-length silhouette by Allison. How proud and poised he looks in full uniform! It took a true artist to give him this look without a hint of haughtiness.

This is a fine cutting. There are slight touches of Chinese white on the figure that have paled out. The interior scene in the background is hand colored.

The silhouette was purchased from the Elizabeth L. Maurier collection.

No. 49
CUT-AND-PASTED FAMILY GROUP
BY PHILLIP LORD OF MAINE

Dated 1835

PRIVATE COLLECTION

Groups of silhouettes forming a single setting are quite rare today. Most of them seem to remain in private and institutional collections.

Phillip Lord has achieved a relaxed family situation with which many of us can identify. The cuttings have animation, as do the faces on the boy and the man singing at the piano.

Chinese white has been added to the silhouettes to enhance the forms and give us a better idea of the clothing and hair styles.

The interior background scene is hand painted in gray water color tones. Every now and then in just the right places, a color is introduced. There are red and yellow flowers with green stems and leaves in the vase, and blue, green, and brown washes appear in the painting on the wall. The background is soft and does not detract from the silhouette forms. This is a very pleasing and successful grouping.

No. 50
FULL-LENGTH, CUT-AND-PASTED SILHOUETTE
BY SAMUEL METFORD

Dated 1843

PRIVATE COLLECTION

Nathaniel Hawthorne is the subject of this superb profile by Samuel Metford. I'd like to think Mr. Hawthorne was this handsome.

The silhouette stands out very well against the painted interior background. The entire design and layout of the piece is artistically conceived and executed.

One notices the figure first and is next drawn to the fireplace, mantle, mirror, and over to the cord, which brings one back down to the figure once again. This is the approach of a talented and well-trained artist. The portrait is signed, dated and you know who the subject is. It is museum quality, unquestionably.

CHAPTER SIX

Conservation and Preservation of Your Silhouettes

by C. R. Jones

MOST SILHOUETTES CONSIST of one or more pieces of paper, with a backing of black paper or fabric. Eighteenth- and early nineteenth-century paper was made primarily from linen rags, which produced a strong, flexible paper resistant to yellowing under normal conditions. Depending on the type of screen used on the paper mold, handmade sheets of paper have a texture of short parallel lines (*laid* paper) or a smoother texture like fine screening (*wove* paper). Wove paper is more commonly used for silhouettes because finer details can be cut from a smoother surface.

After about 1860, more and more paper was made from wood pulp, a material containing lignin and acids that eventually form colored compounds on aging. Paper made in this way will turn yellow and become brittle. A conservator can usually perform washing and deacidification treatments on this paper, but some deterioration continues. This situation is called *inherent vice*—that is, the destructive agents are part of the paper itself.

Other materials may include black backings of laid or wove paper or fabric. These might be somewhat acidic and cause staining on the reverse of the front paper. *Flint* paper—paper coated with a shiny black material—is frequently found as well. These papers are usually not acidic, but the least amount of moisture can cause them to bleed or stick to other papers.

Handling

One of the first principles of preserving a silhouette is to handle it properly. If it is framed, you can remove the glass to examine it. These are the steps to follow.

First, prepare a clean work surface and cover it with a white blotter or heavy, soft paper. Then place the frame face down with enough padding to protect fragile frame parts, if any. Make notes about everything you find. Remove old labels carefully and preserve them. If nails are holding the backing in place, remove them with pliers of an appropriate size, working on the side of the frame farthest away from you and pulling each nail toward you.

If possible, remove the glass, silhouette, and backing together and place them right side up on the table. Check visually, or use a small spatula, to make certain the paper is not stuck to the glass. If it is, seek the advice of a paper conservator. If the glass is free, lift it off and note its orientation in the frame.

Now examine the silhouette itself for tears, discoloration, "foxing" (brown spots), and stains. The silhouette may be loose in the frame, or it may be attached to a black backing paper or to a separate backing board. Adhesives vary a great deal, and it is best not to try to undo them without some special training.

To turn the piece over, place clean blotters or pieces of paper above and below and turn the entire stack. Remember that there often are very delicate cuts in the paper and the edges are easily damaged. Protect the piece from sudden movements or even gusts of air that might sweep it to the floor.

Common Problems

The silhouette may have discoloration (from bad-quality backings or long exposure to light); stains; foxing; large or small tears; faded inscriptions, hair, or costume details; or damaged silhouette paper or fabric. If the mat is poor quality, there may be *mat burn*, a yellowed halo around the opening.

If moisture has condensed inside the frame, or if the piece has actually been wet, yellowish brown stains may show on the paper. As the paper wets unevenly a dark "tide line" often forms. Water stains can be very difficult or impossible to remove completely, but a paper conservator may be able to reduce them to an acceptable degree.

Frames not properly sealed against dust usually collect a considerable amount of surface dirt, even under the glass. A very careful brushing with a soft-bristle water color brush will usually remove it.

Paper conservation is a complex matter with many potential complications, so it is best left to a professional. Paper conservation requires suitable materials, easily reversible adhesives, and cleaning techniques that are tested before use.

Reframing

Acid-free rag board is now available from many framers and suppliers. This is the material that you should use for a *backing* and *window mat*. The backing protects and supports the silhouette from contact with poor-quality materials. The window mat prevents it from touching the glass. Silhouettes are usually quite small and it may be hard to insert a mat of this size, but it is important. Paper in direct contact with glass often sticks to it because of moisture condensation.

A *dust seal* of acid-free, pressure-sensitive paper tape should next be placed around the edges, overlapping the glass slightly in front and the backing in back. If an old wood backing bears an inscription or must be retained, you can preserve it separately or place it on the back of the frame with an isolating layer of mylar film between it and the acid-free board.

After making certain that the frame is secure, insert the taped package in the frame and fasten with brass nails (escutcheon pins) or stainless steel pins. Do not use steel brads, which can rust and cause stains to penetrate the backing.

Never hammer nails into a frame. To avoid the risk of damage, use a *fitting tool*, a device available from framing supply houses, or a *brad pusher*, which you can find at most hardware stores.

Environmental Conditions

The ideal conditions for the preservation of paper are a temperature of about 60 degrees F. and a relative humidity of 50 to 55 percent. Paper is *hygroscopic*—that is, it absorbs moisture from the air when the relative humidity is high, and it loses moisture when the relative humidity is low. Rapid fluctuations may cause the paper to "cockle" or wrinkle. Relative humidities over about 70 percent encourge mold growth, while very low relative humidities cause the paper to become brittle and turn yellow.

Ideal conditions can seldom be maintained in the home, but portable humidifiers or dehumidifiers and sufficient ventilation can reduce fluctuations and extremes. Gradual seasonal changes are usually not harmful.

Strong light will discolor paper and make it brittle, so keep silhouettes out of direct sunlight. Also avoid fluorescent light, which is high in the most damaging ultraviolet rays. Ink or water color inscriptions or embellishments are particularly sensitive to light. Long exposure to almost any light will eventually fade them. Iron gall ink tends to be somewhat acidic and in conjunction with long light exposure can easily destroy the paper fibers.

A safe, clean envrionment will usually prevent paper-eating insects and mold from getting a start; but watch out for them, particularly if the paper gets wet. Insects usually eat enough of the paper to be very evident. Mold starts as a microscopic growth, then appears as white fuzzy spots, and finally starts to digest the paper, causing black stains. Fresh air and brief exposure to sunlight will often kill the growth, but mold spores are in the air and if given enough moisture may grow again.

Conservation Principles

Several rules can be borrowed from the conservator. First, keep good records, both written and photographic, of your pieces. Examine them periodically for signs of trouble. Maintain a fairly even relative humidity and keep them away from strong light. Handle the silhouettes carefully and see that they are framed properly. Retain and record any inscriptions, labels, or information that are important to their history.

If you see a problem that requires a paper conservator, seek his or her advice. Conservators cannot work miracles, but they can often advise you about difficult framing problems and treatments that might improve the appearance of a piece and prolong its life. Paper can sometimes be washed to remove stains, for instance, or even gently bleached using sunlight. It is sometimes advisable to remove old pressure-sensitive tape mends and to repair tears with easily reversible materials. Each silhouette will have different problems and will require a tailor-made treatment.

With some knowledge of the damaging factors we have discussed, a commitment to safe handling and framing, and an awareness of when to seek professional advice, you should be able to maintain your silhouettes in a condition as good as or better than they were in when they came into your hands. Taking care of such a legacy is not an easy task, but it is a rewarding one.

Bibliography

BOOKS

Carrick, Alice Van Leer. *A History of American Silhouettes: A Collector's Guide—1790-1840.* Rutland, Vt: Charles E. Tuttle Co., 1968.

Jackson, Mrs. E. Nevill. *Silhouettes: A History and Dictionary of Artists.* New York: Dover Publications, Inc., 1981.

Worrell, Estelle Ansley. *Early American Costume.* Harrisburg, Pa.: Stackpole Books, 1975.

Rumford, Beatrix T. *American Folk Portraits: Paintings and Drawings from the Abby Aldrich Rockefeller Folk Art Center.* Boston, Ma.: New York Graphic Society, 1981.

CATALOG

For Costume and Hair Styles
Sotheby's. *American Folk Art: From the Collection of Peter Tillou, Litchfield, Conn.* New York: Sotheby's, Saturday, October 26, 1985.